TANIA BECAME A CEO

Tania Kabangu
Tania Became a CEO

Published by BooxAi

ISBN: 978-965-578-292-9

TANIA BECAME A CEO

Never Stop Dreaming

TANIA KABANGU

To all the little dreamers out there, this story is dedicated to you. To the kids who have fire in their hearts and a spark in their eyes, who see the world as a place full of endless adventures, know that anything is achievable as long as you believe, work hard and never give up on your dreams.

TANIA BECAME A CEO

Tania was just a little girl when she discovered her love for cleaning. She would always help her Mom with housework and keep her room clean. She made sure everything in the house was in its proper position.

Tania had big dreams of becoming a CEO of a cleaning company one day. She was determined and didn't let anyone talk down on her dreams. She was fixed on achieving her dreams and her family and friends were always supporting her.

As Tania grew older and started living on her own, her love for clean environments grew stronger. She learned new cleaning techniques and better products and scents to help a home look its best.

Tania began her cleaning business and named it Angoshine (Any Place Good Shine). She started by helping people clean their homes and workplaces. At first, things were not so easy because it was a different experience for Tania. But she never gave up. She kept striving and she put more hard work into her business.

She learned more about how to relate with people and how to manage a business. Soon Tania's hard work began to pay off and some people started to patronize her business. Although she still needed more clients to keep the business running.

PRINCIPAL

Tania was so determined and with the help of advertisement and marketing, her business began to grow stronger. Today, Tania is a successful businesswoman and her cleaning business has grown stronger and stronger.

Angoshine

Her company took care of the cleaning of several houses and businesses like clinics, spas, gyms, high-rise condominiums, hotels, schools and many other places.

Tania became a role model to many young people who saw her as an inspiration. Tania also helped support the community with donations and participated in charities.

Tania knew that her success was not just about making money but also about making a difference in the world and bringing smiles to many people's faces.

Tania remained humble and grateful and continued to inspire others to chase their dreams and make a positive impact in the world. Although Tania is now so successful, she never stops dreaming. She still has dreams of having her cleaning company all over the world.

Angoshine

Tania's big dreams and determination led her to great success. She is a living proof that anything is possible as long as you believe in yourself and never give up on your dreams.

THE END

Afterword

If you believe in yourself and your abilities, you can achieve anything. This sentiment is rooted in the idea that a strong belief in yourself can give you the confidence, determination, and resilience needed to overcome any obstacle or challenge that may come your way.

One of the keys to believing in yourself is to have a positive mindset. This means approaching situations with a can- do attitude and believing that you have the skills and resources necessary to succeed. It also means not letting setbacks or failures discourage you but rather viewing them as opportunities to learn and grow.

Another important aspect of believing in yourself is setting clear goals and working towards them in a systematic and consistent manner. By setting specific, achievable goals, you can give yourself a sense of direction and purpose and track your progress as you work towards achieving them. It is also helpful to surround yourself with supportive people who believe in you and your abilities. Having a strong support system can provide motivation, encouragement, and guidance as you work towards your goals.

Afterword

Ultimately, believing in yourself is about having faith in your own abilities and knowing that you have what it takes to overcome any challenge that comes your way. With this belief, you can accomplish anything you set your mind to.

About the Author

Tania Conde Kabangu is an entrepreneur and an author. She is the Founder of Angoshine International LLC, a licensed professional cleaning company, a vision birthed from her appreciation for a clean environment from childhood.

Tania developed her housekeeping hobby through persistent and intentional efforts. She learned professional cleaning techniques and business management in order to be able to take care of the cleaning of several houses and businesses.

Tania is passionate about writing to inspire children to believe in themselves in order to make their big dreams come true.